Bob Fosse: The Life and Legacy of Decorated Choreographer

By Charles River Editors

Cirencester College, GL7 1XA
Telephone: 01285 640994

About Charles River Editors

Charles River Editors is a boutique digital publishing company, specializing in bringing history back to life with educational and engaging books on a wide range of topics. Keep up to date with our new and free offerings with this 5 second sign up on our weekly mailing list, and visit Our Kindle Author Page to see other recently published Kindle titles.

We make these books for you and always want to know our readers' opinions, so we encourage you to leave reviews and look forward to publishing new and exciting titles each week.

Introduction

Bob Fosse and Viveca Lindfors in the 1963 revival of
Pal Joey

"The time to sing is when your emotional level is just too high to speak anymore, and the time to dance is when your emotions are just too strong to only sing about how you feel." – Bob Fosse

By the turn of the 20th century, American entertainment was still preoccupied with European-style operetta, as embodied in the works of cellist-composer Victor Herbert. Traditional dance forms moved from European stories to the American prairie in Oklahoma by the late 1940s, and what was once the property of Bavarian princes became the singing standards of cowboys riding through the corn fields in *Oh What a Beautiful Morning and Out of My*

Dreams.

In terms of original choreography, it was the age of Jerome Robbins that marked the first real departure from traditional dance on stage and in film. Robbins, born in 1918, became a five-time Tony winner and twice winner of an Academy Award. It was into this environment, featuring his *West Side Story, Fiddler on the Roof, The King and I,* and countless other productions, that an intriguing new choreographer made his entry riding the advent of American jazz. Only 10 years Robbin's junior, Robert Louis Fosse, better known as Bob Fosse, followed his colleague's example by mixing daring new jazz forms with virtually every traditional and popular genre to produce previously unseen modes of dance expression on Broadway and in film.

In the 1960s, Fosse emerged as one of the leading dancers, actors, choreographers, directors, screenwriters and film directors on Broadway and in Hollywood. He became famous for conquering several fields on the musical stage and film simultaneously in a way that no one has before or since. It is said that "only Busby Berkeley compares" to Fosse despite the fact that Berkeley was never a dancer, and that Fosse enjoyed eight Broadway hits to Berkeley's one.[1] Fosse forever changed the way the modern audience viewed dance on stage and

[1] Ed Sikov, Review of Sam Wasson's Fosse, *Film Quarterly*, Vol. 67 No. 2, University of California Press

film. Coupling his rise with the sexual freedom movement, he is known for an "intense, unbelievably driven, provocative, entertaining…sexual, physically demanding" choreographic style.[2] Difficult for even the best dancers, the range of expression encompasses "joyous humor, as well as bleak cynicism."[3]

[2] Ed Sikov

[3] Ed Sikov

The Prodigy

The timing of Bob Fosse's birth coincided with some of the most extreme cultural changes of the 20th century, as reflected in his work, but the location was also crucial to his artistic makeup. He was born June 23, 1927, in the city of Chicago and named after Robert Louis Stevenson, author of his parents' favorite novel, *Treasure Island*. Chicago was the second most important town for theater in America, and all the Western vaudeville circuits had been located there, a fact that was "central to his artistic identity."[4]

Both of Fosse's parents had ties to show business, and his father Cyril and his Uncle Richard played as a vaudeville act around the region. Cyril played the spoons and Richard the piano, with both singing. However, early on in Fosse's life, his uncle was diagnosed with cancer, and Cyril took up a job as a traveling salesman with the Hershey Chocolate Company. Fosse's mother, Sadie, was a spear-wielding regular at the opera as an extra.

The fifth of six children, Fosse was recognized early on as a child prodigy, and the show business leanings of his parents made them aware of it. Despite nagging health problems, he immersed himself in tap from the age of nine, studying at the Chicago Academy Theater under

[4] Travalanche, Bob Fosse: Of Dance, Death and Immortality – www.travsd.wordpress.com/2020/06/23/bob-fosse-of-dance-death-and-immortality/

Frederic Weaver, who would subsequently become his booking manager. The solid instruction he received there was "wide-ranging and vigorous…a professional grounding."[5]

He was already dancing as a professional at the age of 13 as a high school sophomore. Soon, he was half of a quasi-vaudeville act known as The Riff Brothers, in tandem with Charles Grass. Most of the high school performances were held in local strip clubs, "an experience that no doubt colored his later work."[6] It is suggested by author Natalie Barrett in *Practiced to Pro Dance* that the "darker undercurrent"[7] of this experience provided the touch of more sordid aspects of the industry, and of human nature evident in his adult work.

The sum total of Fosse's choreographic palette encompassed the entire offerings of the dance world. He "inherited and handed down"[8] popular dance forms he was too young to have participated in directly, but the still strong residue in the city of Chicago helped him to define them as "classical."[9] He transformed back-alley dance and strip club entertainment into high art, and despite the passing of vaudeville and burlesque well before his time,

---

[5] Travalanche

[6] Natalie Barrett, Practiced to Pro Dance, Bob Fosse Dance Style – The Techniques and Moves You Need to Know, May 6, 2010 – www.practicedtoprodance.com/bob-fosse-dance-style-the-technique-and-moves-you-need-to-know/

[7] Natalie Barrett

[8] Travalanche

[9] Travalanche

he was old enough to be captivated by the classical veterans.

One of his former dancers suggested that many of his influences and perhaps his "entire package"[10] was formed at the feet of Joe "Frisco" Rooney, known as the "Father of Jazz Dance."[11] Rooney is the first individual known to have danced to jazz music, and likely coined the line "Don't applaud, folks; just throw money."[12] His most famous steps consisted of shuffles and contortions, to which Fosse's later examples demonstrate a great similarity. Like Fosse, Rooney used a derby hat and a cigar as props, along with his "deadpan expression"[13] and odd posture. The primary difference between the two is that Rooney's dancing was "erratic and improvisatory,"[14] whereas Fosse's was "highly wrought and pre-conceived."[15] Still, the overall look was strikingly similar.

---

[10] Travalanche

[11] Travalanche

[12] Barbara Quintana-Bernal, Joe Frisco: The First Jazz Dancer – www.vaudeville.sites.arizona.edu/node/39

[13] Barbara Quintana-Bernal

[14] Travalanche

[15] Travalanche

Rooney

At the age of 18, Fosse enlisted in the Navy, but on the day he reported to boot camp, V-J Day was declared and the Second World War ended. He completed two years of duty and returned to New York City, and with the help of the GI Bill, Fosse found it possible to take a year of courses at the American Theater Wing for acting, singing, ballet, modern dance, and choreography. His first show after returning from the Pacific in 1947 was a touring company of *Call Me Mister*, where he met fellow dancer

Mary Ann Niles. They were married for two years from 1949-1951. Niles was Fosse's first real dance partner, with whom he made his New York City debut. The couple also made their Broadway debuts together in *Dance Me a Song* on January 20, 1950, a show that closed after only 35 performances. They appeared together on the *Morey Amsterdam Show* and *Your Hit Parade*. Their activities were rounded out by various professional work in television and stage variety shows, and a few minor Broadway chorus parts. During this time, Fosse put together a few of the classic hallmarks found in his later choreography.

His marriage to Niles ended in 1951, but Fosse's second wife was waiting in the wings. Joan McCracken was also a cast member in *Dance Me a Song*, and she stood out among Fosse's "revolving door of romantic partners"[16] as a relentless salesman for Fosse and his work. While he was notoriously unkind to his former wife and upstaged her at every turn in "a humiliation too perverse to bear,"[17] McCracken trumpeted her husband's virtues to any prestigious director within earshot. Fosse referred to McCracken as "the biggest influence in my life."[18] He marveled at her rate of connectedness within the business, and as the two partied with every influential figure in the

[16] Julie Miller, Fosse/Verdon, The Tragic Story of Bob Fosse's Second Wife, Joan McCracken, Vanity Fair – www.vanityfair.com/hollywood/2019/04/bob-fosse-gwen-verdon-wifi-joan-mccracken

[17] Julie Miller

[18] Julie Miller

industry, Fosse sat anonymously while McCracken took her turn with each celebrity passing by.

McCracken

It was McCracken who convinced Fosse to give up night clubs and go for more prestigious targets. At her insistence, he studied directing and choreography formally, and when she was cast in Rodgers and Hammerstein's *Me and Juliet*, she bandied about Fosse's name whenever director George Abbott came in the room. According to producer Hal Prince, it was McCracken who was "single-handedly responsible for getting Bob Fosse his first job as a choreographer on Broadway."[19]

Abbott

Unfortunately, as Fosse's star rose, McCracken's health declined, even as she had successfully hidden her diagnosis of diabetes. At one point, Fosse allowed her the opportunity to fill in for future wife Gwen Verdon in the starring role for *Damn Yankees*, but when McCracken came to see the show, she realized immediately that she was far too sick to handle the role. The two were divorced

[19] Julie Miller

within five years, and she died of a heart attack barely a decade after their marriage began. In later recollections, Verdon made note of how strong a hold McCracken had over Fosse, explaining, "Years from now, you'll read how Bob enhanced so many lives…not one of us, except Joan, was ever able to enhance his."[20]

Fosse continued with television work on such stalwarts as the *George Burns and Gracie Allen Show*, the *Arthur Murray Party*, and the *Colgate Comedy Hour*, where he received his first television choreography experience, thanks to the patronage of Jerry Lewis. From that distance, he was able to make an in-depth study of Fred Astaire, and from fellow choreographer Jack Cole, whose ethnic Asian underpinnings and male eroticism caused friction with various directors and producers.

Before plunging headlong into a career as a choreographer, Fosse was to enjoy one more big year as a performer. In 1953, he appeared in the films such as *The Affairs of Dobie Gillis,* which starred Bobby Van and Debbie Reynolds. He then appeared in *Give a Girl a Break* in the same year, with stars Marge and Gower Champion, a dance and choreography couple famous for the film *Showboat* and other blockbusters. Debbie Reynolds also co-starred.

---

[20] Julie Miller

1953 ended on a high point for Fosse, as he caught his first big break in *Kiss Me Kate*. There, his brief contribution caught the attention of Broadway masters Jerome Robbins and George Abbott. At the time New York City Ballet choreographer Robbins recommended him to George Abbott, Fosse only had one dance number to his credit of 45 seconds duration. His resume listed other choreography credits, but most were bogus, and they were likely easily seen through by one of Robbins' stature. The "fake it 'til you make it"[21] strategy was not limited to job interviews, as Fosse had to audition constantly to appear in shows, producing "nausea-inducing"[22] anxiety in many cases. His fear of failure was such that he once told the *New York Times*, "If I had to audition on Wednesday, I'd start throwing up on Saturday night."[23]

[21] PBS, Broadway, Bob Fosse – www.pbs.org/wnet/broadway/stars/bob-fosse/
[22] PBS
[23] PBS

Robbins

Early Choreography

In his earliest professional attempts at choreography, Fosse displayed a "dizzying mix of styles."[24] In one show alone, he crafted an alluring world both "artificial and theatrical"[25] with a synthesis of ballet with jazz, marching style with can-can, gypsy dance and traditional British music hall, African dance and vaudeville, "an amalgamation of all these things."[26] He was incredibly

---

[24] Enotes.com, Bob Fosse – www.enotes.com/topics/bob-fosse

[25] Enotes.com

[26] Natalie Barrett

"story-driven,"[27] and always referred to his dancers as actors. From the beginning, directors constantly tried to limit the full expression of his choreography, telling him to tone down the "lewd undercurrents and themes viewed as improper."[28]

Fosse was a perfectionist about detail, and every limb not in use had a function and place. Some of the immediately recognizable features of Fosse's work included turned-in legs with hands cupped, as if holding a soft-boiled egg. This was often coupled with hands to the hips with elbows tucked in and back. Hand movements were constant and wildly articulated, with a sloped back so the body would present a diagonal line. Clicks with snaps of the wrist were common, particularly while keeping the rest of the arm absolutely still. In an anti-ballet position, shoulders were curved, and there was much sideways shuffling. All movement was set against a backdrop of stillness to produce the maximum effect. The parts not moving were of equal importance, creating a "clean minimalist edge."[29]

Needless to say, the difficulty factor was always high, requiring the dancer to be in the best possible condition. One dancer made note of the paradox in Fosse's appeal, describing the general style as "goofy sex."[30] Such an

---

[27] Natalie Barrett

[28] Enotes.com

[29] Natalie Barrett

appearance was made up of oddly juxtaposed angles, isolations, turned-in legs, and a fluidity that combined to create a sex appeal "with a hint of awkward."[31]

Some of Fosse's hallmark characteristics are universal names on Broadway and in Hollywood. In addition to the "soft-boiled egg" hands, a famous one was the "broken doll walk," with feet turned-in and hands hanging loosely on the hips. The vintage "jazz hands," with fingers splayed and hands shaking, was rescued from dance oblivion by Fosse as a new standard for Broadway. The "rake" employed an angled torso with the working leg extended to the front and turned out. The upper-stage hand was affixed to the rim of a bowler hat, while the downstage hand remained on the hip with the elbow tucked in.

In the "crane," one knee was bent to a parallel *retiree*, with the supporting leg also bent on demi-pointe. The torso was contracted, with the head tucked, creating a "C" shape with arms curved back. The "amoeba" was a combination move that included pigeon-toes, finger snaps, shoulder rolls, jazz hands and hip isolations. In what were called "crescent jumps," the legs began in parallel, and one leg came into a "coup" when jumping. The "drip" featured a front leg facing sideways with the torso facing

---

[30] Natalie Barrett

[31] Natalie Barrett

the front. The clbows were tucked to the side with the lower arms extending outward with broken wrists and hands hanging down. The move was called the "drip" based on the idea that if one poured water on the dancer, it would all run off the arms and drip off. In the "slow burn," the eyeline of every dancer shifted slowly from one side of the stage to the other.

The "steamboat" had the dancers standing in an inverted second position (pigeon-toed), and the torso leaning forward and teacup hands on a hat. In such steps, Fosse loved to play with paradox, being "elegant and broken at the same time."[32] The "stack" produced an optical illusion involving multiple dancers. One sat in a chair, while the second dancer fit in front of them, legs together and hands out in second position. The final dancer sat on the lap of the second dancer, and all had fingers splayed. It could also be done from a standing position. In the "linkage," dancers were linked through locked arms, up or down, with elbows bent and fingers splayed. The gesture took place while walking downstage with a slight body roll.

These and other hybrid maneuvers have bled through to the style of Michael Jackson and Beyoncé, and into various styles of film. Prior to Fosse's influence, it was standard practice to shoot the front facing forward, or from an overhead viewpoint. Fosse implemented a host of

[32] Natalie Barrett

other angles, and "jump cuts." His films have become known as "music dramas,"[33] a term derived from Richard Wagner's operas to set them apart from Italian works. For Fosse, they were "musically-oriented films with sophisticated themes amid stark realism."[34]

The first show in which Fosse choreographed the entire production was *The Pajama Game*, released in 1954. It was an overnight success and showcased much of Fosse's trademark choreographic style, including suggestive forward hip thrusts, vaudeville humor with hunched shoulders and turned-in feet, and mime-like articulation of the hands. He often dressed dancers in black with white gloves and derbies à la Charlie Chaplin, complete with pratfalls, sleight-of-hand, and double takes. Fosse received his first Tony Award in Best Choreography in 1955. *The Pajama Game* opened at the St. James Theater on May 13, 1954, running for 1,063 performances and it marked the beginning of Shirley MacLaine's career.

The most notable dance scene in *The Pajama Game* is generally agreed to be the number "Steam Heat," producing a lasting history of Fosse's work. It was recreated in the film two years later and became a staple of MacLaine's nightclub act. The name served as a title for a later documentary on Fosse, which aired on *Great*

---

[33] Enotes.com

[34] Enotes.com

Performances of PBS. Fosse went on to choreograph the film adaptation with Doris Day.

Day

My Sister Eileen was released in 1955, the first film in which Fosse was engaged as a major choreographer. The picture starred Jack Lemmon, Betty Garrett, and Janet Leigh as an adaptation of *On the Town*, a dance-heavy show famous for Jerome Robbins' *Fancy Free* ballet incorporated into the action. Fosse took advantage of the format to create the memorable *Competition Dance* number for himself and Tommy Ball.

Award Winner

On May 5, 1955, *Damn Yankees* opened at the 46th Street Theater, and it went on to be the most successful show of Fosse's young career. Based on the book of George Abbott and Douglass Wallop, *The Year the Yankees Lost the Pennant*, it transferred from the 46th to the Adelphi Theater two years later for a total of 1,019 performances. Also directed by Abbott, it was the first time Fosse was to work with the great Gwen Verdon, a triple threat actor-singer-dancer with a trail of hits over the previous three years. The forming of the Fosse-Verdon alliance was to be of equal importance to the success of *Damn Yankees*, the story of an older man who sells his soul to the Devil to become a professional baseball player. Verdon, above all dancers before and since, "understood his [Fosse's] dance vocabulary, and executed it to perfection."[35]

---

[35] Mark A. Robinson, Fosse/Verdon: The Dynamic Duo of Broadway, Broadway Direct – www.broadwaydirect.com/fosse-verdon-the-dynamic-duo-of-broadway/

Verdon

Still, it was not an easy role for Verdon to win. Initially, Fosse rejected her until he could see how they worked together. In her recollections, Verdon recalled, "I had a reputation for being difficult…and I was. I was difficult because I couldn't stand bad dancing."[36] Verdon played the seductress hired by the Devil to make the rejuvenated baseball player fail and was forever associated with the role. A close relationship soon developed, and the two were already living together by the time Fosse's divorce

[36] Lauren Hubbard, The True Story of Bob Fosse and Gwen Verdon's Relationship, Town and Country –
www.townandcountrymag.com/leisure/arts-and-cultural/a2708914/bob-fosse-gwen-verdon-relationship/

from McCracken was official.

EllaRose Chary of MTI Shows calls the concept of
Damn Yankees "Faust meets baseball."[37] The setting takes
place in 1955, the era of Mickey Mantle and the historic
greatness of the New York Yankees. The oddest number,
and the only existing tape of Fosse and Verdon dancing, is
Who's Got the Pain? It's a quirky number, but
deceptively cheery. It was a "weird"[38] last minute
replacement for a number performed in a gorilla suit that
Fosse liked but the rest of the creative team hated. It was a
piece of film demonstrating that "Fosse wasn't always a
genius…one of the stupidest songs in any Broadway
musical…completely unnecessary to the plot."[39] Still,
Damn Yankees is one of few shows in which fantasy
translates well.

Julie Miller of *Vanity Fair* declared somewhat tongue-in-
cheek, "If you exclude the bedroom part, they [Fosse and
Verdon] were loyal to each other their entire lives."[40] The
Wasson biography traces Fosse's womanizing back to an
incident in which he was molested by a group of strippers
at the age of 13 in a burlesque hall where he worked.
Miller further observed that Fosse "didn't demean

[37] Ella Rose Chary, MTI Shows, in Literature: DAMN YANKEES, May 9, 2011 – www.mtishows.com/news/mto-shows-in-literature-damn-yankees

[38] The Verdon/Fosse Legacy, How They Met – www.verdonfosse.com/history

[39] Rational Magic, Damn Yankees – www.rationalmagic.com/Bursting/DamnYankees.html

[40] Julie Miller, Vanity Fair, Inside Bob Fosse and Gwen Verdon's Unconventional Marriage, April 9, 2019 – www.vanityfair.com/2019/04/gwen-verdon-bob-fosse--marriage

sensuality in his dance style…but had a lot of anger toward women."[41]

Fosse and Verdon were well aware of the other's skills, although their paths had never crossed. She was an established star, and he was an up-and-comer. Verdon had even worked as a junior choreographer, taught in a dance school in Beijing, and served as dance coach to Jane Russell and Marilyn Monroe. That, however, did not stop Fosse for asking to work with Verdon for an entire day before offering her the role. Then, according to Hal Prince, he had the audacity to call the office and ask for several days more. Verdon went for it, likely realizing that she would do the same thing in his place. Miller suggests that she saw "a crumpled, soft-talking dance tramp, and that he saw the sweetest, hottest dancing comedienne of the age."[42] It may be that what actually made Verdon "difficult" is that it was the 1950s, and she had opinions about dance, calling the normal Broadway jumping around style "animated wallpaper."[43]

No one knows what happened over those few days, but "the synergy that manifested had a profound impact on both careers."[44] Verdon claimed that the character of Lola was Fosse's in its entirety, including "the flirtatious

---

[41] Julie Miller

[42] Julie Miller

[43] Julie Miller

[44] The Verdon/Fosse Legacy

quality, the accent, when you push your hair back, when you breathe…blink…move your little finger."[45] Their stage work not only produced a Tony for each of them in *Damn Yankees*, but over the years, they combined to win 13 Tony awards, four Drama Desks, three Emmys, one Academy Award, one Cannes Film Festival Award, and one Grammy.

In the following year, Fosse choreographed *Bells are Ringing* with Judy Holliday on Broadway, in partnership with Jerome Robbins. The show ran for a total of 924 performances and was nominated for Best Choreography to both Fosse and Robbins. The story is based on a woman who runs an answering service and the characters she meets there. It opened at the Shubert Theater on November 29, 1956, and had a successful run based in part on the heavy dance component and the Jule Styne score. The romantic comedy was far removed from Fosse's later works and showed little of the customary distress caused by his later staging.

Fosse choreographed *New Girl in Town*, which opened in May 1957 at the 46th Street Theater, and ran for 431 performances. It was based on O'Neill's play from the 1920s, *Anna Christie*. The book was written by George Abbott, about a prostitute trying to live down her former life. Fosse was eager to highlight new star Gwen Verdon,

---

[45] Julie Miller

hot off a successful run of *Damn Yankees*, but nothing about the book lent itself to large dance routines. A "Cathouse Ballet" in *New Girl in Town* was cut in Boston and producers burned the scenery in the alley behind the theater to prevent it from being restored. Fosse was nominated for Best Choreography, and Verdon won another Tony.

Scarcely had the set been struck from *New Girl in Town* that Verdon and Fosse began work on *Redhead*. A "sexy murder mystery" set in London around the 1880s, the time of Jack the Ripper, the show set out to prove that mysteries could do well as musicals. Opening in 1959, with Fosse in charge of staging, *Redhead* won six Tony Awards, including Best Musical. It featured Verdon and marked a debut of sorts for Fosse, who had never been so intimately involved with all of the stage work. He naturally transformed the bulk of the show into a "dance-heavy"[46] production. In the rare case of a woman having written the book, Dorothy Fields broke through as an author. The idea was shopped around to stars such as Ethel Merman and Bea Lillie but sat on the shelf until it caught the attention of Fosse and Verdon.

Redhead ran for 452 performances, but in the decades following its success, it has been classified as a critical failure. It has never been revived, none of the songs went

[46] Mtishows.com, Redhead – www.mtishows.com/redhead/

on to become hits, and there has never been a film adaptation. Some ascribe its haul of Tony awards to the fact it ran during a weak season, but it did beat out Rodgers and Hammerstein's popular *Flower Drum Song*. Furthermore, critics were nearly unanimous in the belief that Fosse's staging "elevated the mediocre material into an exhilarating evening."[47]

Verdon and Fosse were married in 1960, and the beloved Broadway star and the dazzling new choreographer soon introduced their new daughter Nicole to the public, evoking a wide range of reactions. Growing bolder with each new success, Fosse's struggles increased with directors and producers who wanted him to tone down or remove "controversial"[48] parts of dance routines. He realized that if he was to continue to develop, he needed to be the director as well as choreographer. At a time in which a sexual freedom movement was sweeping America, he and Verdon created a string of the most famous musicals and films of their era, and they soon became established among the most famous dance and choreography duos in Broadway's history.

Fosse and Verdon were of similar artistic personalities as "highly creative, driven people."[49] Unfortunately, their

---

[47] Diane Bertolini, The Lost Musicals: Redhead, New York Public Library, 2012.11.13 – www.nypl.org.blog/2012/11/13-lost-musicals-redhead

[48] PBS, Broadway

[49] Lauren Hubbard

goals and desires often clashed in dramatic fashion, exacerbated by the fact that Fosse was a notorious philanderer. On the side, he took up many vices borne of nervous anxiety, including smoking and the abuse of prescription drugs. As for Fosse's womanizing, Verdon pointed out that Fosse "grew up around strip clubs. Women were his hobby. He'd even cheat on his mistress. Part of him felt guilty, another part was ecstatic."[50]

1961 found Fosse directing and choreographing *Conquering Hero*, a musical version of Preston Sturgis' *Hail the Conquering Hero.* Based on a book by Larry Gelbart, Fosse was released from the production during the previews due to an argument with the author over the direction of the book. It was during a rehearsal of *Conquering Hero* that he first experienced a public seizure, leading to his diagnosis of epilepsy. The show only ran for eight performances starting on January 16, 1961. Featuring Tom Poston and Lionel Stander, Fosse's name went uncredited, and he was replaced as director by Albert Marre and by Todd Bolender as choreographer.

How to Succeed in Business Without Really Trying was choreographed in 1961, with the film version to come six years later. It was co-choreographed by Fosse and Hugh Lambert, although Lambert's contribution was reportedly "minimal."[51] The show opened October 4, 1961 and ran

---

[50] Lauren Hubbard

for 1,417 performances.

Nicole had been born during Fosse's work on *Little Me*, based on a Neil Simon play, and she would grow up to serve as co-executive producer of a famous documentary entitled *Fosse/Verdon*. The original 1962 production was impressive, with Sid Caesar playing multiple roles with multiple stage accents, both husbands and lovers.

Two years later, Fosse played the lead, directed, and choreographed in a Broadway revival of Frank Loesser's *Pleasures and Palaces* on Broadway. The show was a rare musical comedy flop on Loesser's part. The title is borrowed by an internal line in the song *There's No Place Like Home*, and the story was based loosely on the career of American naval hero John Paul Jones. This was somewhat ironic since Jones had joined the Russian navy following the American Revolution, and *Pleasures and Palaces* came at the height of the Cold War. *Pleasures and Palaces* was to open in March 1965 at the Fisher Theatre of Detroit, starring Phyllis Newman, but Loesser did the unthinkable when he "pulled the plug."[52]

One theory as to why Loesser abandoned the show was that he was expecting his second child and would rather have been home. An alternate theory suggests that he

[51] Frank Loesser.com, How to Succeed In Business Without Really Trying – www.frankloesser.com/library/how-succeed-in-business-without-really-trying/

[52] Jerome Weeks, Pleasures and Palaces – Lyric Stage Revives a 'Lost' Broadway Musical, *Art and Seek*, Dec. 26, 2012

knew what he was dealing with and knew that it wasn't going to work. A third notion suggests that Fosse had stuffed the show so full of choreography, despite much of it being thrown out, that it simply couldn't be ready in time. Loesser remarked that "Fosse put an awful lot of dancing in it."[53] The Lyric in Chicago made an attempt to revive the musical since the scripts and orchestral parts had not been thrown away, which was quite unusual for productions that didn't make it to New York.

In 1966, Fosse and Verdon opened *Sweet Charity* together. Based on another Neil Simon script, Verdon won a Tony, and Fosse won the Tony awards for Best Director and Best Choreographer. It opened on January 29, 1966 at the Palace Theater, and it had a run of 608 performances in New York. The story is centered around a New York "taxi" dancer who is unlucky in love until she meets "a strait-laced claustrophobe"[54] and nurses him through a jammed elevator incident.

A musical adaptation of the Fellini film *The Nights of Cabiria*, a French film, *Sweet Charity* is one of Bob Fosse's first major shows as both director and choreographer. Verdon claims that the two of them accidentally saw the Fellini film, and that it "made an

---

[53] Jerome Weeks

[54] Mark Robinson Writes, Sweet Charity, Broadway Musical Time Machine: Looking Back at Sweet Charity – www.markrobinsonwrites.com/the-music-that-makes-me-dance/2016/11/10-broadway-musical-time-machine-looking-back-at-sweet-charity

indelible impression"[55] on Fosse. Unable to sleep that night, he produced an entire outline for a new musical adaptation by the following morning. Fosse bought the rights to make a libretto from Fellini for a sum of $25,000, and he invited Neil Simon to collaborate.

The production was nominated for awards in nine categories but won only one. It was also a failure at the box office, albeit representing a triumph for Fosse himself as he had created a popular new style of dance to vulgar jazz in a cabaret setting. *Sweet Charity* was later filmed with Shirley MacLaine taking Verdon's role. MacLaine refused to shoot it unless Fosse directed, and Verdon helped the film production in numerous capacities but went uncredited.

---

[55] Mark Robinson

A scene from the "Big Spender" dance routine in the film version of *Sweet Charity*

One reviewer called *Sweet Charity* a "hymn to female resilience."[56] The most well-known number is "Hey, Big Spender" for a line of veteran hookers who have become emotionally detached in order to do their jobs. According to reviewer Mark Robinson, *Sweet Charity* was conceived by Fosse as a vehicle for Verdon, and "doesn't work without a strong choreographer helping to tell the story, and an amazing dancer in the lead."[57] It is actually a dance piece, Robinson writes, "occasionally interrupted by the

[56] Concord Theatricals.com, Sweet Charity – www.concordtheatricals.com/p/44690/sweet-charity

[57] Mark Robinson

pesky conventions of musical theater (speaking and singing)."[58] As for the pure choreography, it is "a ballet about the heart and a modern dance about the mind."[59] Vernon possessed all of the empathetic qualities required for the role, and was unsurpassed as a dancer, but the same cannot be said of everyone who has played her since.

For Fosse, "innovative dance" often meant the inclusion of "the oldest stripper tricks in the book."[60] All the countless nights of conducting "research" at the clubs paid off in *Sweet Charity*. "No one was ever just part of the chorus."[61] He typically created a feature of style out of people's shortcomings, even Verdon's. She suffered a case of Ricketts as a child and was knock-kneed, a trait that is incorporated into her choreography for *Sweet Charity*. In the same show, Fosse choreographed an extended number known as the "Rich Man's Frug." An American dance craze during the '60s that evolved out of the "twist" and the "chicken," Fosse used it with perfect timing, demonstrating the "Aloof," the "Heavyweight," and the "Big Finish." The number explains perfectly the character of each person, just by the way they walk and stand.

[58] Mark Robinson

[59] Mark Robinson

[60] Move Your Story, "The Rich Man's Frug" by Bob Fosse: A Short Dance History Lesson, Feb. 16, 2018 – www.moveyourstory.org/stories/2018/2/10/the-rich-mans-frug-by-bob-fosse

[61] Move Your Story

Due to a series of Fosse's extramarital affairs, Verdon and Fosse separated in 1971, but they never quit working together and were never officially divorced. They continued to collaborate on such hits as *Chicago*, *All That Jazz*, and *Cabaret*, for which Verdon traveled with Fosse to Europe to assist with filming.

Cabaret was released in 1972 and won Fosse the Oscar for Best Director. Based on Christopher Isherwood's stories about early 20th century Germany, the subject matter touched a nerve overseas. Articles appeared all over Germany, with prominent photos displayed in *Time* and *Newsweek*. It was nearly guaranteed to be a huge public draw while still in the conception stage.

At the same time, *Cabaret* represented the trappings of a sexual horror story, featuring a female sexuality that was "warped and monstrous"[62] in its era. It bared an all-encompassing homophobia within Nazi culture, protesting effeminacy as a mere signifier of the evils of the Nazis. It insists that an entire culture is responsible for the historical atrocities, not merely a single political party. The audience's mood is thus changed from a political one to an internal reality that is much more frightening. Further complicating the intricate mind game is the gender confusion that keeps viewers off-balance

[62] Linda Mizejewski, Women, Monsters, and the Masochistic Aesthetic in Fosse's Cabaret, *Journal of Film and Video*, Vol. 39, No. 4, *Spectatorship, Narrativity, and Feminist Revision* (Fall 1987)

whenever they try to sympathize with various characters. The social impact of *Cabaret* comes from the fact that it was filmed during the Vietnam War and replaced pleasurable viewing with a "masochistic aesthetic."[63]

Whether Fosse's adaptation was a "faithful" one is difficult to pin down, as *Cabaret* had such a circuitous origin. The source material was Isherwood's *Goodbye to Berlin*, a series of short stories. The '72 film was an adaptation of a musical produced six years earlier, which was an adaptation of a novel published a quarter century prior. The modern film of *Cabaret* is not to be confused with the film released in the'50s, which is an adaptation of a play produced four years earlier. With all the diverse directions taken with the Isherwood, it can still be consulted, penned just before the Second World War, and published in the midst of it. Among the most compelling lines from the original was "I am a camera,"[64] which became the title of the first stage adaptation, giving both readers and audience members a "cannily voyeuristic"[65] feeling. This adaptation handled the risqué subject matter with "glee and disgust,"[66] right up Fosse's alley.

Cabaret starred Liza Minelli, the young and dashing Michael York, Helmut Griem, and Joel Gray as the

[63] Linda Mizejewski

[64] Keith Schnabel, Is Bob Fosse's Cabaret An Unfaithful Adaptation, June 5, 2020, Medium – www.medium.com/@keithschnabel/is-bob-fosses-cabaret-a-faithful-adaptation-28e968fbbf33

[65] Keith Schnabel

[66] Keith Schnabel

specter-like Master of Ceremonies. Fosse learned of the project taking shape in 1971 from the director of the original production, producer Harold Prince, and he won the director's position after some fierce political backroom fighting. Increasingly dissatisfied with Jay Presson Allen's script, he hired Hugh Wheeler, commonly known as a "research consultant," to rewrite it. The new book transformed into a "sharp political satire"[67] through the lens of Fosse's own "off-kilter sensuality."[68]

[67] Christina Smith, Bob Fosse, 'Cabaret' and the Performer's Eye for Filmmaking, March 28th, 2019, Film School Rejects – www.filmschoolrejects.com/bob-fosse-cabaret/
[68] Christina Smith

Minelli in the film

Fosse's close collaboration with the film's editor, David Bretherton allowed him to "realize his dream of total control of every stage element, toe, tap, and facial expression."[69] Bretherton realized that Fosse had a rhythm that "lent itself well to long days in the cutting room."[70] He had positioned the cameras generally from a low angle looking upward at the stage performers, enhancing one's

[69] Christina Smith
[70] Christina Smith

feeling of being spectators, then made rapid cuts from wild dancing to a "mannequin-like audience."[71] Small physical gestures took on enormous power, such as when Sally Bowles "literally stops time"[72] with nothing more than an inverted knee.

Fosse never thought he would win an Academy Award for his work in *Cabaret*, but in the end, the show won eight, including Best Director, a total triumph in reclaiming his reputation. Much like his leading female character, "to perform was the crux of his life,"[73] rewarded or not.

Among the most disturbing scenes in *Cabaret* was the dancing gorilla, accompanying the text "If you could see her through my eyes, she wouldn't look Jewish at all."[74] That line was softened before the final cut, but the point was still clear. The character of Sally Bowles was based on English screenwriter and activist Joan Ross, well known to Isherwood. She fought her entire life to distance herself from the character. Minnelli naturally brought a professionalism to the character as a performer, but in the original, the lead female was intended to be a shy neophyte trying to get a break in a cabaret. Fosse changed Sally Bowles to an American in order to recruit Minnelli,

---

[71] Christina Smith
[72] Christina Smith
[73] Christina Smith
[74] Keith Schnabel

whose disturbed character mirrored the effects of Fosse's own womanizing. Six numbers in the original score were dedicated to an elderly romance between Fräulein Schneider and Schulz. They were not written by Isherwood, and Fosse cut all but one.

Pippin, which opened in 1972, became the highest paid Broadway musical to advertise on national television, and Fosse won the Tony Award for the Best Director and Choreography. Music and lyrics were provided by Stephen Schwartz, with a book by Roger O. Hirson. Fosse also contributed to the libretto about the son of Charlemagne, Holy Roman Emperor, and his search for fulfillment. Fosse had toyed with realism in *Cabaret* to great success.

The outward appearance of *Pippin* has produced a reputation as being "harmlessly naughty,"[75] but when performed as Fosse intended, it is "surreal and disturbing."[76] Most viewers do not immediately sense the "depth of meaning and subtext."[77] At first reading, Fosse did not like the show, believing it to be too "cute and sentimental."[78] As an antidote, Fosse created the Leading Player, or the narrator, and the Best Buddy. These two characters controlled every event to make sure that Pippin

[75] Scott Miller, Inside Pippin, New Line Theater – www.newlinetheatre.com/pippinchapter.html
[76] Scott Miller
[77] Scott Miller
[78] Scott Miller

failed at everything he tried. Ultimately, they attempted to influence him into fulfilling their version of a "grand finale" by immolating himself.

Fosse turned *Pippin* into something "dark and cynical."[79] The original happy ending was traded for a compromise, while the rest was transformed into a "parade of frightening, disturbing incidents in which Pippin finds less and less satisfaction."[80] Absolutely no one connected with the show liked Fosse's changes, or the eventual style of setting, but it nevertheless opened in October 1972.

Fosse felt that he was constantly dealing with a show that possessed a weak musical score. His solution was to have the script and accompanying music ridicule itself. The dialogue makes fun of the upcoming *Corner of the Sky*, sung by Pippin as an inane example of juvenilia. The "Grand Finale," despite not resulting in Pippin's self-immolation, was nevertheless "genuinely bizarre."[81] When Catherine asks Pippin how he feels, Pippin replies "Trapped…but happy."[82] Fosse cut the last half of the line. Neither the composer nor John Rubinstein, who played Pippin, liked that choice. However, Fosse was not only the director, but quite intimidating. After the run ended, Schwartz put the line back in.

---

[79] Scott Miller
[80] Scott Miller
[81] Scott Miller
[82] Scott Miller

As he had in other shows, Fosse employed many styles of choreography, most notably the "jazz hands," declaring that "I don't hesitate to lift from every form of American show business."[83] He and Schwartz were a poor fit, and he told the *New York Times*, "We fought all the way. I think he's very talented. But not as talented as he thinks he is."[84]

The quick changes of concept and tinkering with the book showed in the reviews. Clive Barnes of the *New York Times* wrote that "the book is feeble and the music bland, but the show runs like a racehorse."[85] After nearly 2,000 performances, *Pippin* closed six years later. Rubinstein, despite disapproving of Fosse's changes, claimed in retrospect, "I love that man. I felt we were on the same wavelength, even though we are of different generations."[86]

Fosse invented the Broadway television ad for *Pippin*, which helped it to survive the mixed reviews. It consisted of Ben Vereen dancing with two girls, with no razzle-dazzle or special effects behind, except shot from every conceivable angle. The group was called the "Manson Trio," as Charles Manson was big in the news of the day as a "pied piper."

[83] Laurie Johnston, Fosse Discusses Creation of Pippin, New York Times – www.nytimes.com/1972/11/07/archives/fosse-discusses-creation-of-pippin.html

[84] Laurie Johnston

[85] Andrea Simakis, John Rubenstein, the Original Pippin Remembers Bob Fosse, Broadway's First TV Ad, and Irene Ryan Bringing Down the House., Cleveland, Plain Dealer, June 30, 2015 – www.cleveland.com/onstage/2015/01/john_rubenstein_the_orioginal_p.html

[86] Andrea Simakis

On September 10, 1972, Liza Minnelli, fresh off a long run of *Cabaret,* released a variety show-style concert special for NBC entitled *Liza with a Z.* It was directed and choreographed by Fosse, with Marvin Hamlisch as conductor, and according to Minnelli during a later revival, "It was the first filmed concert for network TV ever done."[87] The show was accomplished through the use of eight cameras before a live audience, with one run-through only. The show's numbers included several from *Cabaret.* Minnelli was 26 at the time and at the top of her game.

For his part, Fosse credited Joan McCracken for steering him toward the Broadway stage and film, explaining that she had told him, "You're too good for night clubs."[88] Fosse, terrified of failure, was honest in an interview with David Sheehan, who filmed Fosse's production of *Pippin.* He observed that despite all the success, he didn't believe he possessed the intelligence or talent to pull off new projects: "Every time I start on something new, it's like day one. How do I do this?"[89] Despite the feeling that he had simply gotten lucky each time or pulled the wool over someone's eyes, he followed McCracken's advice faithfully, and never looked back. *Liza with a "Z"* won the Emmy for Best Choreography and Overall Outstanding

[87] Karu F. Daniels, Liza Minnelli's Liza With a Z Concert to Air on PBS in August, NY Daily News – www.msn.com
[88] PBS
[89] Ellen Gutoskey

Directorial Achievement in Comedy, Variety or Music.

Fosse made an increasingly rare appearance as a dancer himself in *The Little Prince*, which opened in 1974. A space traveling child prince roams a new planet searching for fulfillment, encountering many strange animals along the way. Fosse danced the role of a derby-wearing snake, with moves that can be found later in Michael Jackson's work. Biblically based, the movie version of *The Little Prince* is of questionable suitability for young children. As the title would suggest, as the snake kills him in the end.

Also in 1974, Fosse directed a biopic of the controversial and pioneering comedian Lenny Bruce, starring Dustin Hoffman. Fosse had recently entered a mental health rehabilitation center, and all around him were concerned when he took up *Lenny*. His behavior on set was to make for a "tense atmosphere"[90] when mixed with Hoffman's own antics as an *enfant terrible* and a generally low-energy script. Hoffman and others took issue with Fosse's "perfectionist tendencies"[91] and multitude of takes. In a *Rolling Stone* interview at the time, one crew member declared, "The guy's overrated and he knows it…knows the critics will be gunning for him, so he's trying to cover

---

[90] Caitlin Gallagher, All the BTS Drama 'Fosse/Verdon' Fans Should Know about that Lenny Bruce Biopic, Bustle – www.bustle.com/e/bob-fosses-lenny-biopic-with-dustin-hoffman-won-a-ton-of-awards-but-earned-the-director-a-bad-on-set-reputation-17875723

[91] Caitlin Gallagher

his ass."[92] The general complaint among the cast came to be known as the "Fosse bitch."[93]

In the end, *Lenny* did garner some acclaim. It was nominated for six Academy Awards, including Best Director for Fosse and Best Picture, but it lost out to *Godfather, Part II*. When asked about the best part of making the film, Hoffman replied, "When it was over…a very depressing shoot."[94] For Fosse, the film did his health no good, and he lapsed into increased drug use, with related health problems. *Lenny* marked the beginning of the end for Fosse's movie career, and he would only make two more, *All That Jazz* and *Star 80*.

In 1975, Fosse was editing *Lenny* and rehearsing *Chicago* at the same time. Soon after he had assembled the cast, he suffered a heart attack during the first week of rehearsal and was rushed to the hospital, where he underwent open heart surgery. In his absence, the cast was miraculously held together, but upon his return, his mood had significantly darkened. Death had been a caricature for Fosse up to that point, but now it was real. Lyricist Fred Ebb habitually referred to Fosse as the "Prince of Darkness." The medical incident had changed him, and in a significant way, it changed the nature of the show.

---

[92] Caitlin Gallagher
[93] Caitlin Gallagher
[94] Caitlin Gallagher

Chicago was based on a true story from the 1920s, citing the cases of two women who killed their partners and got away with the crimes. It opened in 1975 at the 46th Street Theater and ran for 936 performances. However, in a testament to its continued relevance, it eventually surpassed *Cats* with its 7,486th performance in the West End.

Fosse turned *Chicago* into a "scathing satire"[95] on show business and the media, which created "celebrity criminals."[96] Filled with raw sexuality, it created a frightening world in which it was fashionable for women to kill lovers and husbands and subsequently be rewarded with instant fame. By the time it opened, Fosse had created the most "savage"[97] satire since Brecht and Weill's *Threepenny Opera*.

Like *Cabaret*, *Chicago* was designed to make the audience uncomfortable, and Fosse saw to it that it "never tempers its cynicism with compassion."[98] Fosse always maintained that *Chicago* was his answer to Watergate, and it has maintained relevance through the years, as evidenced by its extended performance schedules. The issue in the original book of the 1920s was alcohol. In Fosse's version, the issues consisted of prayer in school,

[95] Scott Miller, Inside Chicago, New Line Theater – www.newlinetheater.com/chicagochapter.html
[96] Scott Miller, Inside Chicago
[97] Scott Miller, Inside Chicago
[98] Scott Miller, Inside Chicago

sexuality, and marriage, but the model is the same.

It was Verdon who talked Fosse into doing the show, and he responded instantly to setting it in the vaudeville age. Starring Verdon, Chita Rivera, and Jerry Orbach, the stage was never without high tension, and Fosse made some rare reversals along the way. The song "Razzle-Dazzle" simulated sex on both sides of the stage while the lawyer spoke of "flimflamming"[99] the courts and the public. Fosse was convinced to restage the song in a toned-down version. The song "Class" was too offensive, and Fosse censored the original version. Others were cut from the later film.

Despite some troubles, *Chicago* arrived in New York in good shape. It received 11 Tony nominations, but it lost all of them to *Chorus Line*, which practically swept that year's awards. However, its popularity was only belated for a short while. Fosse knew vaudeville like virtually no one else in his generation and reveled in it, with a "profound distrust in show business."[100] Roxie Hart was one of the most interesting characters ever created by Fosse. He gave her "greater moral (or amoral) heft…[as] a child-woman"[101] than the others. Fosse showed an almost uniform aversion for real emotion, to the point of being comical. Mr. Cellophane, the only pure character, was a

[99] Scott Miller, Inside Chicago
[100] Scott Miller, Inside Chicago
[101] Scott Miller, Inside Chicago

perennial loser. To Fosse, he represented the American people, who kept losing. To Fosse, "We're the real suckers."[102] Fosse's message was that publicity "subverts justice"[103] as courtrooms become circuses with cameras creating a new breed of celebrity.

Fosse acted in a film version of Herb Gardner's *Thieves* with Marlo Thomas and Charles Grodin in 1977. His next stint with a musical came with *Dancin'* a year later. Set on Broadway as a musical revue, Fosse won the Tony Award for Best Choreography, as an answer to the success of *A Chorus Line*. In his attempted return to Broadway in the same vein, the show was dance-laden and sparse of dialogue.

Dancin' opened with Fosse's girlfriend Ann Reinking in the lead and closed four years later after 1,774 performances. The show was nominated for seven Tony Awards, including Best Musical. In an eclectic evening, Fosse married "high intensity, varied dance styles"[104] to a soundtrack of J.S. Bach and Neil Diamond.

[102] Scott Miller, Inside Chicago

[103] Scott Miller, Inside Chicago

[104] Mark Kennedy, Bob Fosse's 'Dancin' plans to glide back to Broadway, ABC News, June 3, 2021 – www.abcnews.go.com/Entertainment/wirestory/bob-fosses-dancin-plans-glide-back-to-broadway

Reinking

Nicole Fosse, who helped organize a revival years later, objected to the production being called a revue. She was adamant that although it had "no plot, you are taking on a specific journey."[105] She added that the Fosse style had not been adequately represented in the interim, growing "stagnant, over-posed and two-dimensional,"[106] where it should be "broad and eclectic."[107] No recording of the original production exists, but Nicole possessed a large quantity of source materials and extensive notes taken by

[105] Mark Kennedy
[106] Mark Kennedy
[107] Mark Kennedy

her father.

It may be that in *All that Jazz*, released in 1979, Fosse reached the height of his film career, both in directing and choreography. Once more in a nod to the influence of Fellini, Fosse dismissed any notion of impropriety by exclaiming, "When I steal, I steal from the best."[108] In this quasi-autobiographical depiction, Fosse turned the camera on himself, depicting a driven choreographer who edits one show while rehearsing another, all with the aid of pills, booze, and sex. *All That Jazz* features Audrey Paris, reportedly a character based on Verdon. Actress Jessica Lange, with whom Fosse was rumored to have had an affair, plays the director's girlfriend in the film. The story picks up around the time that Fosse experienced his first heart attack.

Fosse implied that in all our lives, there was "no reality outside of the imagination that conceives it and the mind that produces it."[109] For Fosse, life was an individual experience, each person "chipping off raw chunks of matter from the mine of subconscious impressions, spilling chemical and genetic colors onto them, and churning it all into consciousness."[110] The story of *All That Jazz* was "lived, conceived and experienced through one person's head, heart and nervous system."[111] It is a

---

[108] Ellen Gutoskey

[109] Alvin J. Seltzer, "All That Jazz": Bob Fosse's Solipsistic Masterpiece, Literature/Film Quarterly Vol 24 No. 1 (1996)

[110] Alvin J. Seltzer

world of sensationalism, "no matter how hard and honestly it does strive for depth, truthfulness, and respectability." As its chief character declares, "To be on the wire is life. Everything else is waiting."[112]

According to Alvin J. Seltzer of *Literature/Film Quarterly*, "He feels death bearing down on him if he waits a second too long,"[113] and he must keep everything spinning. Seltzer cites Angelique, Gideon's partner, as the ideal image of death, dressed in "the tradition of his profession…like a combination bride and showgirl."[114] As a professional, Fosse was never able to control his addiction to women, but in the art, he "turned personal tragedy into an aesthetic triumph."[115] At the death of the director/choreographer, Fosse took away all the artistic props, except for a truncated Ethel Merman rendition of *There's No Business Like Show Business.*

Beside the autobiographical element, the source material for *All That Jazz* has been likened to Fellini's *8 ½,* "obsessed and exhausted."[116] The director drives himself to death in a search for success. The search for innovation in the dancing was a constant, and Fosse observed that "Today, I get very antsy watching movies in which people

---

[111] Alvin J. Seltzer
[112] Alvin J. Seltzer
[113] Alvin J. Seltzer
[114] Alvin J. Seltzer
[115] Alvin J. Seltzer
[116] Enotes.com

are singing as they walk down the street…you can do it on the stage."[117]

Alternate influences aside, this "madly imaginative, self-excoriating musical masterpiece"[118] remained true to Fosse's style and to his routine of "amphetamines, booze, and sex."[119] Coming from the darkest period of Fosse's life, the action nevertheless retained a high state of energy throughout with dancers such as Ann Reinking, Leslie Palmer, and Ben Vereen. Auditions were so strict that Reinking was forced to audition several times for a role based on herself. Daughter Nicole, then 16, appeared briefly as a Principal Dancer. At one point, Fosse considered playing the lead himself, but it was pointed out by producer David H. Melnick that he would likely not survive the shoot, having just had a heart attack.

The character of Angelique was based on Fosse's McCracken, and the relationship between the choreographer Joe Gideon and Victoria Porter was based on the relationship between Fosse and dancer Jennifer Nairn-Smith from their days at working on *Pippin*. Nairn-Smith actually appeared in the production, and virtually all other cast members had an autobiographical connection to Fosse.

[117] Enotes.com

[118] Criterion Collection, Bob Fosse, All That Jazz – www.criterion.com/films/28561/all-that-jazz

[119] Criterion Collection

Usually review neutral, *Britannica*'s Michael Barson suggested that the production was a "self-indulgent though hardly self-serving autobiographical film."[120] He added that the notable dance numbers and strong script were frequently "interrupted with hallucinations about death."[121] While the baring of Fosse's soul was fascinating, it became "difficult to watch."[122]

All That Jazz drew great acclaim. It was nominated for nine Academy Awards, including Best Picture, and it won the Oscar for Best Director and Best Original Screenplay. The production garnered much praise among fellow directors as well. Stanley Kubrick reportedly called it "the best film I think I've ever seen."[123] The last musical number, "Bye-Bye Life," which one called Fosse's "ode to dying,"[124] is among the most powerful musical numbers in the history of film.

The production was the first to appear in the VHS format with a stereo soundtrack. It took 101 days to shoot, and post-production ran for eight months. It was the final movie directed by Fosse, and *All That Jazz* won the Palme D'Or Award at the 1980 Cannes Film Festival.

Roy Scheider is generally thought to have played Gideon

[120] Michael Barson, Bob Fosse, American Choreographer and Director, Britannica, June 19, 2021 –
www.britannica.com/biography/Bob-Fosse#ref12000000
[121] Michael Barson
[122] Michael Barson
[123] IMDB, All That Jazz – www.imdb.com/title/#0078754/trivia
[124] IMDB

extremely well, and he worked so hard that he actually looked like a dancer, but he was not. When he chose dancers early in the film, he wore an earpiece connected to Fosse so as to appear to know what he was doing. Despite being a chain smoker, Fosse was forced to give Scheider coughing lessons, and off-camera, an assistant director held a knee against Scheider's chest during takes. Many were considered for the role of Gideon. Some were too British, others too old, but the most interesting candidate was Warren Beatty. He stipulated, however, that he would not take the role if the character died at the end.

Al Auster of *Cinéaste* took exception to the selection of Roy Scheider for the main role, and to his character development. No hint of Gideon's origins could be found in his actions or a rationale for his pathologies. Since he was not a dancer, "Fosse therefore loses whatever chance he had to reveal character through song and dance."[125] Auster offered a general view that although modern directors were attempting to bring heavier messages, Fosse "confuses message with self-absorption."[126] He reminded readers that Richard Rodgers died in the same month as *All That Jazz* was launched, and despite all the controversial works he wrote, the audience never heard a word about him personally.

[125] Al Auster, Reviewed Work: All That Jazz by Robert Alan Arthur, Bob Fosse, *Cinéaste* Vol. 10, No. 2 (Spring 1980)
[126] Al Auster

The budget blew up from $6.5 million to over $10 million, and at one point Columbia refused to give the project any more money, despite being unfinished. Fox financed the rest of the show for top billing over Columbia, and it was a good choice, as *All That Jazz* became the only R-rated musical to ever be nominated for Best Picture at the Academy Awards. Brandon Sparks of Medium suggested that *All That Jazz* "exudes a type of confidence that wasn't fully present in the previous films of Fosse. Of course, the primary theme of the film was 'excess.'"[127]

In 1983, Fosse tackled a subject of which no one wanted any part, a biopic of Canadian playmate Dorothy Stratten and her murder at the hands of a jealous husband. Controversial at the time, *Star 80* earned nominations for several awards as a non-musical crime drama. It offered a retelling of the young model's last days before she was murdered by her husband, Paul Snider, who then turned the gun on himself.

This last major film of Fosse's starred Mariel Hemingway, Eric Roberts, and Cliff Robertson. The American biographical drama was based on Teresa Carpenter's *Death of a Playmate*, and on Stratten's brief life. Fosse was relentless in his research, undertaken three years following the crime. He studied autopsy reports,

---

[127] Al Auster

obscure interviews with Stratten herself, and spoke with anyone who knew either her or her husband. He scouted locations in Vancouver, British Columbia, and Los Angeles, where Stratten lived and worked, adding them to the film. Actual quotes were incorporated into the dialogue, and to avoid litigation, Fosse was required to document the source of virtually every scene and dialogue exchange in the script.

Star 80 could not hope to match the energy of the similarly grisly subjects of *Chicago* and *All That Jazz.* The dark underbellies of those cultures were "alive with performance and theatricality."[128] *Star 80* was set in the drab world of auto shows, wet T-shirt contests, and playmates roller skating in bikinis "for the delectation of male celebrities."[129] In *Blissing Out: The Politics of Reaganite Entertainment*, Andrew Britton wrote that 35 years after its release, *Star 80* remains "a bracing and clear-eyed examination of a young woman's exploitation."[130] The film explores the thesis statement of female eunuch Germaine Greer, that "women have very little idea of how much men hate them."[131] *Star 80* was not genre material like the other films, despite being based on "the stuff of demented horror – a terrifying…descent

[128] Roger Ebert.com, Christina Newland, A Horror Story for Our Times: Another Look at Bob Fosse's "Star 80": Nov. 15, 2016 – www.rogerebert.com/features/a-horror-story-for-our-times-and-another-look-at-bob-fosses-star-80

[129] Roger Ebert.com

[130] Roger Ebert.com

[131] Roger Ebert.com

into the red mist of misogyny."[132] Fosse traced the behavior of three men who tried at every turn to "market, control, and possess Dorothy for their own ends."[133]

Star 80 was not a horror movie, but it has still been called "one of the scariest films of its decade."[134] Fosse's film made literal what typical slasher movies made "metaphorical."[135] Backlash came to Fosse as being too similar to his on-screen villain. He did not help matters by implying that he would have been similar to the murderer had he not succeeded in show business. That Fosse made any attempt at all to humanize Snider, the husband, was generally off-putting, particularly in the age of awakening to celebrity abuse of women. Even where it was admired, the movie was intensely disliked in all quarters. Critics and audiences "hated Fosse's ice-cold approach to celebrity madness."[136] One critic recalled a first screening where the audience's revulsion was audible. Since Fosse examined the circumstances of the murder three years after the fact, there was time enough for audiences to have moved on to the all-too-common next psychopath, but *Star 80* was one of the most honest films created in ages. It represented a rare occurrence where a director understood his material exceedingly well, but in the end,

---

[132] Roger Ebert.com

[133] RogerEbert.com

[134] RogerEbert.com

[135] Roger Ebert.com

[136] CT News, Star 80: Bob Fosse's Hate Letter to Show Biz, May 27, 2018 – www.ctnews.com/2018/05/27/star-80-biob-fosses-hate-letter-to-show-biz/

very few wanted to watch "what we do to women in the name of entertainment."[137]

Fosse's Legacy

In 1983, Michael Jackson approached Fosse with the idea of choreographing *Thriller*. The exciting new genre of music videos might have attracted Fosse at a younger age, but he rejected the invitation despite the perfect opportunity to employ the Fosse dance style in a high-profile production. Fosse had other things on his mind, and it seems he was aware of the limited time he had remaining to produce a few more projects. That same year, he told *Rolling Stone* about the sobering effect of his first heart attack and opined that given his family history, he only had time for two or three more projects.

In *Big Deal* (1986), Fosse extended his dream of total control over a production by not only directing and choreographing, but in writing the actual book. It would end up being the last work before his death. In lieu of a new music score, Fosse employed pop songs from a wide range of eras, with examples of Ray Henderson, Eubie Blake, and Jerome Kern. *Big Deal* was based on the Italian spoof *Big Deal on Madonna Street* by Mario Monicelli, and the story was centered on a group of incompetent thieves in 1930s Chicago. The show went on

---

[137] CT news, Star 80

to garner five Tony nominations, and Fosse won for Best Choreography. It would be his ninth and final Tony. Critics declared that the production "revels in the big delights of Bob Fosse's choreography. The dancers leap, gyrate, and slither with grace and abandon."[138] Fosse directed the adaptation of the book and amplified the script with over 20 songs.

At the age of 60 in 1987, Fosse and Gwen Verdon were on their way to opening night for a revival of *Sweet Charity* when he collapsed on Pennsylvania Avenue in Washington, D.C. He had suffered this heart attack shortly before 6:30 p.m., and he was taken to George Washington Hospital, where he was pronounced dead at 7:32.

The curtain had gone up on *Sweet Charity* a half hour earlier, and when Cy Colman, composer of the show's score, could not find Fosse, he went out to look for him at his hotel. Gwen Verdon later told him that at first Fosse "felt faint, and finally his knees buckled. She couldn't deal with it and called an ambulance."[139] Cast members learned of Fosse's death around 10:00 p.m. after a final curtain and standing ovation. Before his death, there was no sign that he had been ill, and he was said to have been in "high spirits."[140]

---

[138] John Beaufort, Big Deal: Fosse's Back on Broadway" Pop Song Oldies Propel Musical, Christian Science Monitor – www.csmonitor.com/1986/0416/Ideal.htm

[139] Charles W. Hall and Douglas Stevenson, Bob Fosse Dies After Collapse, failure of the Big Deal on D.C. Street, Washington Post, Sept. 24, 1987 – www.washingtonpost.com/politics/1987/09/24/bob-fosse-dies-after-collapsing-on-dc-street/85aaf6d6-e440-402c7bd29oce10d3/

The *New York Times* published a slightly different obituary, suggesting that Fosse collapsed in his hotel room and intimating that he may not have been on his way to the performance at all. Morton Gould, President of the American Society of Composers, Authors, and Publishers announced Fosse's death that night at a cast party at a local grill.

At the end of his life, Fosse showed a reticence to return to Broadway. He remarked that he wouldn't go back for a while because he felt "still bruised from his greatest failure, the mammoth musical *Big Deal*."[141] The show had been a critical and financial flop, and he added, "It still kind of hurts too much."[142] Fosse had added a strange quirk to his will, providing $25,000 to be split evenly among 66 friends, then to be donated back to a funeral party budget.

Fosse's work on Broadway continued through a handful of his greatest disciples. A revival of *Chicago* was staged in 1996 by Ann Reinking, his last romantic partner. She also adapted and revived his choreography for *Fosse*, which ran between 1999 and 2001.

The Los Angeles Dance Awards was renamed the Fosse Awards after his death and are now known as the

[140] Charles W. Hall, Douglas Stevenson

[141] Charles W. Hall, Douglas Stevenson

[142] Charles W. Hall, Douglas Stevenson

American Choreography Awards. Following his passing, a three-part revue premiered on Broadway in 1999, and a stretch of Paulina Street in Chicago was renamed Bob Fosse Way. He was posthumously awarded a Laurence Olivier Award for Best Theater Choreographer with Ann Reinking. A fellowship in Fosse's name was established by his daughter Nicole at the Alvin Ailey American Dance Company in 2003, and he was inducted into the National Museum of Dance's Mr. and Mrs. Cornelius Vanderbilt Whitney Hall of Fame in 2007.

The most extensive biography of Bob Fosse was penned by Sam Wasson, who interviewed nearly 300 of the artist's friends and associates. What Wasson uncovered was a streak of modesty in the insistent director/dancer/choreographer. According to the author, Fosse admitted to being "a very good craftsman, the best butcher on the block."[143] Then he added with a wink, "Well okay, I'm a master craftsman."[144]

Wasson's biography spans a prodigious 723 pages, but the work is not so overwhelming because of its length. Rather, it is inundated with "story after story of sexual harassment of nearly every woman he encountered over the course of his life."[145] When he suffered his first heart attack, the nurses of the hospital reportedly met on how to

[143] Ed Sikov
[144] Ed Sikov
[145] Move Your Story

treat him without being hit on. According to Wasson, he "crammed his dances so full of sexual imagery, so harsh and loveless that you can't help wondering what made so successful a womanizer."[146] Fosse is said to have "pursued lead dancers and actresses relentlessly,"[147] to the point that one had to beat him up to make him stop. Wasson made it clear that in his opinion, Fosse was "one sick puppy…an emotional disaster."[148]

Wasson further wrote that Fosse was hypersensitive to being bald, and that was why he used hats as props so frequently. However, there has been some disagreement over that theory. Colleagues claim he was not hiding under hats, or he wouldn't have lifted them so freely and so often. In fact, they say that he loved hats because they called attention to the most important feature of his choreography, the head.

Regardless of his concern over his hair, or lack thereof, Fosse suffered through a state of depression much of the time. He "liked to joke about death and dying, but he was completely serious."[149] He was a regular patient of Dr. Clifford Sager and took a habitual mix of Benzedrine and Seconal to address his mood swings, balancing precariously up and down.

---

[146] Move Your Story

[147] Move Your Story

[148] Ed Sikov

[149] Emma Dibdin, Who Was Bob Fosse? 6 Things to Know Before Watching Fosse/Verdon, Harper's Bazaar, April 9, 2019 – www.harpersbazarr.com/culture/film-tv/a27056186/bob-fosse-facts-fosse-verdon/

Fosse directed five films in all and was "not your typical dancing golden boy."[150] Still, he was a genius at turning flaws into assets, including poor turnout and posture. He was known to slouch, so he recreated new styles with these flaws, and he threw in canes, bowler hats, chairs, etc. as props. It has been suggested that his use of gloves comes from a general dissatisfaction with his hands.

A splendid tribute opened in 2019, co-produced by daughter Nicole. Wasson cited Sam Rockwell's masterful performance as the "multi-faceted maniac"[151] in *Fosse/Verdon*. Nicole claims that it was indeed difficult to go through the whole thing again in order to stage the show, which was full of "lies, lovers, drugs, breakdowns and the inexorable onrush of death."[152]

Fosse/Verdon premiered April 9, 2019 and represented an ideal demonstration of how Fosse and Verdon had turned putting on a show into "an art, a neurosis, and a way of life."[153] As Sarah L. Kaufman of the *Washington Post* put it, "Nothing stopped them…Fosse's pill habit, depression, heart attacks…revolving bedroom door or the collapse of their marriage."[154]

Nicole noted that as his daughter, there was "so much

[150] Natalie Barrett

[151] Travalanche

[152] Sarah L. Kauffman, Lies, Drugs, Cheating and All That Jazz: Nicole Fosse Opens Up About Her Famous Broadway Parents, Union Leader, April 13, 2019 – www.unionleader.com/nh/arts-and-ent/

[153] Sarah L. Kauffman

[154] Sarah L. Kauffman

intellect and humor…love and joy"[155] that it was often difficult to identify how difficult the struggle was. Her family dynamic had "a complete lack of clarity."[156] She secured one dancing spot in *All That Jazz*, where she played a dancer stretching out in front of the vending machine and was asked to get out of the way by the director. She spent a great deal of time helping her mother, and working on the Verdon/Fosse Legacy, protecting her parents' intellectual property. According to Nicole, the scene at which her father ends up in a psychiatric hospital, just after winning an award for *Cabaret*, was particularly difficult.

Nicole recalled that as a child, she was constantly told that her father was exhausted from overwork and needed a rest. However, she realized at such times, "We usually go to Acapulco. You don't go to a place like that if everything's going well."[157] She was forthcoming when explaining that a lot of shame surrounded her father's mental health. She realized only later the number of facts "hidden from her, prettied up or manipulated."[158] In retrospect, given the sexual harassment claims, Nicole freely admitted that while Fosse was "a loving family man, there's that other stuff. He was a complete contradiction."[159] Verdon and Fosse knew that their time

---

[155] Sarah L. Kauffman
[156] Sarah L. Kaufmann
[157] Sarah L. Kauffman
[158] Sarah L. Kauffman

together was almost up, and despite their divorce, they were together on an almost constant basis. The principle had been drilled into Nicole by her mother that one must never "postpone things. If you want to be with somebody, do it 'cause they could be dead tomorrow."[160]

Through it all, many consider Fosse to be "the quintessential jazz choreographer."[161] Indeed, there never was or has been a shortage of dancers who wanted to work with him or on his style. In *Dancin'*, he managed to audition 2,000 dancers for only 16 spots. Ben Vereen remarked in his book's foreword that "to have worked with Bob Fosse is to have had your hand directly on the pulse of life,"[162] not to mention a prodigious resume point.

Dancer and writer Mindy Aloff gives a hint as to where Fosse's power came from: "Paradoxically, his dances connect with and excite audiences because the very austere technical requirements that restrict the dancer's body…are suggestive of psychological or cultural repression."[163] In personal terms, Fosse likened his own progression to that of a production's development: "I'm still working on my life, just like it's out of town, and when I get it fixed, I'll bring it in."[164]

[159] Sarah L. Kauffman

[160] Sarah L. Kauffman

[161] Cathy Young, Review: Hand on the Pulse: Dancing with Bob Fosse, Reviewed Work: The Fosse Style by Debra McWaters, *Dance Chronicle*, Vol. 32 No. 1 (2009) Taylor & Francis, Ltd.

[162] Cathy Young

[163] Cathy Young

[164] IMDB

Online Resources

Other books about 20th century history by Charles River Editors

Further Reading

All Musicals, Sweet Charity Review – www.allmusicals.com/sweetcharity/review.htm

Auster, Al Reviewed Work: All That Jazz by Robert Alan Arthur, Bob Fosse, *Cinéaste* Vol. 10, No. 2 (Spring 1980)

Barrett, Natalie, Practiced to Pro Dance, Bob Fosse Dance Style, The Technique and Moves You Need to Know, May6, 2010 – www.practisedtoprodance.com/bob-fosse-dance-style-the-technique-and-moves-you-need-to-know/

Barson, Michael, Bob Fosse, American Choreographer and Director, Britannica, June 19, 2021 – www.britannica.com/biography/Bob-Fosse#ref12000000

Beaufort, John, Big Deal: Fosse's Back on Broadway" Pop Song Oldies Propel Musical, Christian Science Monitor – www.csmonitor.com/1986/0416/Ideal.htm

Bertolini, Diane The Lost Musicals: Redhead, New York Public Library, 2012.11.13 – www.nypl.org.blog/2012/11/13-lost-musicals-redhead

Chary, Ella Rose, MTI Shows, in Literature: DAMN YANKEES, May 9, 2011 – www.mtishows.com/news/mto-shows-in-literature-damn-yankees

Concord Theatricals.com, Sweet Charity – www.concordtheatricals.com/p/44690/sweet-charity

Criterion Collection, Bob Fosse, All That Jazz – www.criterion.com/films/28561/all-that-jazz

CT News, Star 80: Bob Fosse's Hate Letter to Show Biz, May 27, 2018 – www.ctnews.com/2018/05/27/star-80-biob-fosses-hate-letter-to-show-biz/

Daniels, Karu F., Liza Minnelli's Liza With a Z Concert to Air on PBS in August, NY Daily News – www.msn.com

Ebert, Roger, Christina Newland, A Horror Story for Our Times: Another Look at Bob Fosse's "Star 80": Nov. 15, 2016 – www.rogerebert.com/features/a-horror-story-for-our-times-and-another-look-at-bob-fosses-star-80

Enotes.com, Bob Fosse – www.enotes.com/topics/bob-fosse

Loesser, Frank.com, How to Succeed In Business Without Really Trying – www.frankloesser.com/library/how-succeed-in-business-without-really-trying/

Gallagher, Caitlin, All the BTS Drama 'Fosse/Verdon' Fans Should Know about that Lenny Bruce Biopic, Bustle – www.bustle.com/e/bob-fosses-lenny-biopic-with-dustin-hoffman-won-a-ton-of-awards-but-earned-the-director-a-bad-on-set-reputation-17875723

Gutoskey, Ellen, 15 Fascinating Facts about Bob Fosse, Sept. 11, 2019 – www.mentalfloss.com/article/598131/bob-fosse-facts

Hall, Charles W., and Stevenson, Douglas, Bob Fosse Dies After Collapsing on D.C. Street, Washington Post, Sept. 24, 1987 – www.washingtonpost.com/politics/1987/09/24/bob-fosse-dies-after-collapsing-on-dc-street/85aaf6d6-e440-402e7bd29oce10d3/

Hubbard, Lauren, The True Story of Bob Fosse and Gwen Verdon's Relationship, Town and Country – www.townandcountrymag.com/leisure/arts-and-culture/a2708914/bob-fosse-gwen-verdon-relationship/

IMDB, Bob Fosse, (1927-198710 – www.inmb.com/name00002080/

IMDB, All That Jazz: The Filmography of Bob Fosse – www.imdb.com/title/#0078754/trivia

Johnston, Laurie, Fosse Discusses the Creation of Pippin, New York Times – www.nytimes.com/1972/11/07/archives/fosse-discusses-creation-of-pippin.html

Kaufmann, Sarah L., Lies, Drugs, Cheating and All That Jazz: Nicole Fosse Opens Up about her Famous Broadway Parents, Union Leader, April 13, 2019 – www.unionleader.com/nm/arts-and-ent/

Kennedy, Mark, Bob Fosse's 'Dancin' plans to glide back to Broadway, ABC News, June 3, 2021 – www.abcnews.go.com/Entertainment/wirestory/bob-fosses-dancin-plans-glide-back-to-broadway

Miller, Julie, Vanity Fair, Inside Bob Fosse and Gwen Verdon's Unconventional Marriage, April 9, 2019 – www.vanityfair.com/2019/04/gwen-verdon-bob-fosse--marriage

Miller, Scott, Inside Pippin, New Line Theater – www.newlinetheatre.com/pippinchapter.html

Miller, Scott, Inside Chicago, New Line Theater – www.newlinetheater.com/chicagochapter.html

Move Your Story, Fosse's Darker Legacy: Bob Fosse, Ben Vereen, and #MeToo, March 12018 – moveyourstory.org/blog/2018/2/10/fossemetoo

Move Your Story, "The Rich Man's Frug" by Bob Fosse: A Short Dance History Lesson, Feb. 16, 2018 – www.moveyourstory.org/stories/2018/2/10/the-rich-mans-frug-by-bob-fosse

Mizejewski, Women, Monsters, and the Masochistic Aesthetic in Fosse's Cabaret. *Journal of Film and Video*, Vol. 39 No. 4, *Spectatorship, Narrativity, and Feminist Revision*

Mtsishows.com, Redhead – www.mtsishows.com/redhead

PBS, Broadway, Bob Fosse – www.pbs.org/wnet/broadway/stars/bob-fosse/

Quintana-Bernal, Barbara Joe Frisco: The First Jazz Dancer – www.vaudeville.sites.arizona.edu/node/39

Rational Magic, Damn Yankees – www.rationalmagic.com/Bursting/DamnYankees.html

Robinson, Mark A., Fosse/Verdon: The Dynamic Duo of Broadway, Broadway Direct – www.broadwaydirect.com/fosse-verdon-the-dynamic-duo-of-broadway

Robinson Mark A., Sweet Charity, Broadway Music Time Machine: Looking Back at Sweet Charity – www.markrobinsonwrites.com/the-music-that-makes-me-dance/2016/11/10/broadway-musical-time-machine-looking-back-at-sweet-charity

Schnabel, Keith, Is Bob Fosse's Cabaret an Unfaithful Adaptation, June 5, 2020, Medium – www.medium.com/@keithschnabel/is-bob-fosses-cabaret-a-faithful-adaptation-28e968fbbf33

Seltzer, Alvin J., "All That Jazz": Bob Fosse's Solipsistic Masterpiece, *Literature. Film Quarterly*, Vol. 24 No. 1 (1996)

Sikov, Ed, Review of Sam Wasson's Fosse, *Film Quarterly*, Vol. 67 No. 2, University of California Press

Simakis, Andrea, John Rubenstein, the Original Pippin, Remembers Bob Fosse, Broadway's First TV Ad, and Irene Ryan Bringing Down the House, Cleveland Plain Dealer, Jan. 30, 2015 – www.cleveland.com/onstage/2015/01/John_rubenstein_the_original_p.html

Smith, Christina, Bob Fosse, 'Cabaret' and the Performer's Eye for Filmmaking, March 28th, 2019, Film School Rejects – www.filmschoolrejects.com/bob-fosse-cabaret/

Sparks, Brandon All That Jazz: The Filmography of Bob Fosse, Medium.com, July 8, 2020 – www.medium.com/cinenation_show/all-that-jazz-the-filmography-of-bob-fosse

The Verdon/Fosse Legacy, How They Met –
www.verdonfosse.com/history

Travalanche, Bob Fosse: of Dance, Death and
Immortality –
www.travsd.wordpress.com/2020/06/23/bob-fosse-death-
and-immortality

Weeks Jerome, Pleasures and Palaces – Lyric Stage
Revives a 'Lost' Broadway Musical, Art and Seek, Dec.
26, 2012

Young, Cathy, Review: Hand on the Pulse: Dancing with
Bob Fosse, Reviewed Work: The Fosse Style by Debra
McWaters, *Dance Chronicle* Vol. 32 No. 1 (2009) Taylor
& Francis Ltd.

Free Books by Charles River Editors

We have brand new titles available for free most days of the week. To see which of our titles are currently free, click on this link.

Discounted Books by Charles River Editors

We have titles at a discount price of just 99 cents everyday. To see which of our titles are currently 99 cents, click on this link.

Printed in Great Britain
by Amazon